In the Time of Rabbits

Valerie Lynch

In the Time of Rabbits

© Valerie Lynch

First Edition 2019

ISBN 978-1-907435-78-2
Valerie Lynch has asserted her authorship and given her permission to
Dempsey & Windle for these poems to be published here.

Front cover photograph ©Valerie Lynch

Published by Dempsey & Windle
15 Rosetrees
Guildford
Surrey
GU1 2HS
UK
01483 571164
dempseyandwindle.co.uk

A CIP record for this book can be obtained from the British Library

For my son

Rooms

He makes rooms for young men
who have survived their fourteen years,
their years of drowning.

Pulls them   wrecked
from the ravenous sea,
and makes them rooms for safety.

Rooms in which to enquire,
give names to their fears
the fears of childhood

and clothe them for today.
They make friends and nearly friends,
whose words are not those

of parents or uncles who know best.
He hears vibrations in the air,
and turns them inside out.

Contents

The Shape and me

Me, the sand and Auntie Doris,
Auntie, safe and round and comfortable.
On the sand with me.
Holding the painted metal shape
hard and gritty with sand,

I turned it round and round
then made it change the sand
from flat and wet into a cockle shell.

I had made something different from before.
I didn't realise this was changing me.

In the Time of Rabbits

Rabbits came out from the trees
scattered in urgent rushings
now here, now there;
left the burdock swaying behind -
priests absorbed in prayer.

All things were possible
and waiting to be lived.
The grass was silent and slow,
and the sun
rarely spoke at all until after mid-day.

Changing the World

The sky goes walking down the road;
in puddle after puddle
it follows the boy exactly step by step.

He stares as a brief wind romps,
and changes his world

Looking is different from seeing

Look, there's a cow
calls my mummy. I know
cow. It made a huffle noise
the other side of the hedge that time
I had strawberry ice cream.

I know cow
in my picture book too.
It's brown and white and it has
a pinned-on tail.
I can't see cow.

My mummy is pointing.
I can see sky and trees
and one, two fields and
then a sort of bundle
of brown and white.

I want to make her pleased
that I see cow. But I don't.
I know cow.
Look! she says again
and I can feel tears at

the back of my eyes.
I try very hard, but
I only see this brown
and white.
That isn't cow. I know cow.

I think I'll run off
and play.

Word-hunter

1.

who are you?

I am the man
who sets traps in the treetops
to catch tomorrow, before
it slides down the shadows
into the early sun

to file it securely
in dark stone beds
before the grasses find their gleam

I snare the words
that fall between my toes
down rifts in the beds
where I lie

a single osprey flies
in an empty sky

2.

I run the green bog-grass
and tread the marshland sun
in pools where it flames
and drowns

I spin down my net
to catch the words
that fall in the black sleeps of night
before the sun drops in
and strangles them.

Sausages

The houses all laughed when mother sent me
back to the butcher's shop. Now everyone
in the street would know how stupid I am.

I told you HALF a pound, she said,
with us standing there in the road.
And this time, get the proper change!

I put the sausages on the slab
and stared up at the butcher
who looked bulgy and big.

Bigger than Dad.
He leaned right over at me.
His whiskers smelt a bit bad,

so I held my breath.
'Yes, my little dear? You back again?'
Trying not to breathe, I chopped him up,

minced the bits, and stuffed them
in sausage skins. Put mum in too,
then took her out quick. She often

sees my thinks. Then I banged my stick
all the way down the butcher's railings
as I went home.

The Stranger called, will you come?

He led me through places with swithering names
he led me to Toller Porcorum
Pottle Oysters Watery Way
and on to Timeshift Moor

where the sun went down in a gas-lamp light
to the east of the kitchen range
and came up
the north side of breakfast.

This is not a chair

The designer had in mind
elegance, form and function
in one polypropylene chair.

We had in mind our son
aged three
and a rusty cheap old van.

We bolted in the legless chair,
William's gleeful throne
and set off to France.

A holiday for three.

       *

Inside the tent, bluer
than Mediterranean skies,
the chair received once more

its dignity of legs.
It's mine, said Will
pelting his chair to the waves.

Not *a chair* he yelled
as he set off to distant shores.
Full of pasta, cake and

ice cream, William
announced that he loved
mummy and daddy

and much much most
his chair.
My almost-ex got up in a rush

and walked away
down the beach, his back
firing signals

I didn't know how to read.

The Other Girl

A button-hole
stitched precisely on a small piece of cloth.
Callowland School. 1912. Aged 11 years.
Careful stitches
tight and neat
that might prevent the *otherwise,* never exactly seen
but always known.

She had enough to eat;
oil lamps held off the dark.
Except for the corners
where *otherwise* might be.

The girl slid inside the picture
that hung above her bed:
the Lady with Lavender
standing willowy, long-hair falling
at her cottage door.

The gagged mouths of dark
waited
inside her head.

The soldier back from the trenches
also did not want to know
anything any more.
He saw the girl
walked into her picture
and drowned.

He married her,
put her inside his camera,
standing willowy,
long hair falling
by an old wooden bridge.

They lived carefully
only made friends who lived
in the suburbs of dream.
It is possible
that *otherwise* never returned.

Reading a photograph

Is it a taxi, or a bus, its handle hidden by ribbons?
The open door is waiting at the kerb where
Mother can just be seen behind her red roses.

Oh happy day, her wedding dress and her wedding smile –
untroubled, guileless child. I think she's delighted
with my father, his six foot length so upright, stiff,

his pin-striped suit and bowler hat, his smile so tense
and fixed that his cheeks must ache.

I can see Mother, seated inside the car leaning out
to wave goodbye, frightened a little as the wedding faces

move away and lose their loving significance.
I see her turning now to Father, believing he'll know.

And Father's face, still holding his aching smile.

Frost

I know it has always been better
once before –
but really, really it was
when we were seven

and better still at being worse –
as we woke in the bare chill room
our noses frozen as stiff
as Jack Frost's ferns

and sea-horse whorls drawn new
on the single thin window-pane.
Out there in the street someone
had lifted a lid and let in the light.

Barefoot

She's barefoot on rocks
backdrop of surfing pines.
I look at her photograph

amazed at mother so young, so vivid,
so unaware of her nineteen years
of innocence, and of my sorrow

that I wasn't there to see.

The Strawberry Fields

Beyond the woods
in the Strawberry Fields
sun-bright with young birch
and dappled with wild strawberries.

Disposed with care or a rug
(waterproofed) Mother presided;
with cushions, tea-pot and fine china cups
she held her small court.

Dad hovered.
Smiling, she received
my handful
of daisies and dandelions.

The kettle sang carefully
around her head. The flowers and I,
dad and the kettle's song
were anxious to please.

Perhaps
we brought her some rest
from the artillery
that garrisoned her smiles.

Their First House

The falling years
have silenced the house of childhood,
arresting its urgent bodies, father and toddler joy.
Absences lie in wait in every room.

In parloured chill the piano has lost its voice
and mother has walked reluctantly out of the door.
Was she singing? Her song did not want to die.

Possession

That day,
standing deep in summer grass
she held a poppy's scarlet intensity
in one hand. Immersed, alone.

With one brief click of his camera,
he imprisoned her on film.
As the shutter moved home, he looked up.
She was still there. Outside.

Mother waited alone

Dad, you'd have been so upset
if I hadn't tagged you around
followed up trees and cliffs

while Mother waited alone
on a waterproof rug
with a book and a kettle for tea

never asking to come with us -
and I never wondered why
just decided she didn't care.

I think she felt so little entitlement
that she sat quietly back
and let you take me away.

The German Boy

My father went Over the Top
bled through rolls of wire
where the German boy

stared at dad's bayonet
and held out his hands
Father told me this bedtime story

when I was seven or so.
I took over the burden
of those hands, the voice

with no sound. Carried them
over the years, the hands still
desperately reaching.

Handhold

I remember Eden, with kites of yellow
and scarlet ready for flight, and father's
fist clamped tightly over mine.

I look at my hand – it's too big now to fit
where it once felt safe to soar up and into
the blue; yours has shrunk and twisted

beyond the grasp of mine. How can we
have worn our lives so long that we cannot
manage a simple grasp of two hands?

Father had gone to War

We took the long-distance train to the Irish Sea
through rocks and crags to her childhood.
She ran the full length of the shore,
laughing and trailing brown seaweed

into the waves and out.
I'd never seen her before.
I watched the tide reach slowly,
carefully in and across the sand.

Others

In dusking woods we wandered,
and sang in the dark.

Suddenly
a far-off voice alighted in our song,
astounding evidence of others in our world.

Boy

I know you're standing there outside the door
shivering wet and cold.
You must be the brother I'd always wanted.

Quietly, quickly I slide downstairs to smuggle
you in. You slot straight into my world.
We turf out shorts and shirts I borrowed or stole
to turn myself into a boy.

We laugh; you're home at last.
When the big girls knock me down, when
Dad discovers me nicking the Christmas fruit,
I hear you telling me what a boy would do.

We don't have that long. I watch my body change.
Mum buys me a bra.
One day you grip my shoulders, tell me
it's time to choose.

I cry and call until I draw you in.

The earth is awake

Grandmother sang in the bedside dark:
'you must never call on the dead, for they are
the ancestors – they'll welcome you home

to their hearth and offer you feasting and song –
then they will wrap the hills around your bones.'
At my mother's hearth it was never feasting

or song, so perhaps I'll call on the clans
and sing as they fold me into the hills;
and I shall be warm and welcomed tonight.

Granny T's kettle

Granny T, in her two up two down
cold scullery out the back
called them 'sookies'.
Rounded and sootbound from the kitchen range

the sooky sat over its glow. Burped
and hissed until it was time for tea.
Dared you to pick it up without a holder.
I wished very hard that I lived with Granny T.

Out the back

A small lopsided gate
held up by string
Anyone there?
In through the blanket

that warmed the door, past dark places
past china ornaments someone
has to dust,
out the back to a world

that belongs to me
small girl in sensible shoes
through to the high-fenced path
running between The Backs

along along breathless excited scared
through unlit passage between
two houses and onto the road
skip jump rush to the gate.

Just in time.

Grandma wasn't often seen in 22 Garfield Street

Most of grandma lived in the briskness of Dorset hills
those bare-backed horses maned with grass outside Powerstock.
Here she was born. Watched for adders under her feet

and friends who lay in the grass, talked to them in Dorset biscuity chunks.
Worked with the sun's fat clock
that ticked when it wanted and never published regulations.

Marigolds

I don't know why
I think of marigolds.
There were always marigolds
on grandmother's path

growing impatiently
and out of their proper place;
jaunty, orangely vivid
in unexpected patches of dusty earth.

The King James Bible

The Bible sits heavy on its shelf
enclosing on its first page, my mother
(herself so confined and enclosed)

presented at Callowland School
for five years' perfect attendance.
'Perfect'. I could not quite grasp that.

Coughs, colds, diarrhoea, or
just the miseries, pushed quickly
through the front door by Granny T.

'No good you sitting round here,'
when I was nine and off school ill.
I asked, 'What happened *then*?'

'In Assembly', she said, 'I fainted
once or twice a week.' 'And *then*?'
'And then they carried me out.

What a nuisance, they said.' 'But *why*?'
She gave me a look I didn't understand.
'That's how it was,' she said.

The buttonhook

She sat in Gran's armchair,
eyes tightly shut
as everything else was banging

and shouting and tables and chairs
and all Gran's sad belongings
were hustled out of the door.

Her mother took over gran's
needlework box. In one corner,
the girl found Gran's silver

buttonhook, and stole it away.
Her fingers soothed its silver circles
and whorls. Perhaps they were

magic. The girl never spoke of it again.
But the silver buttonhook now belongs
inside her needlework box.

A line of sight

A line of sight links my mother

to father's other beloved
possession, his camera
and arrows on through fifty years
of her death as I remember

a different mother.

Grandfather

Muscles rise as he rolls his barrels from cart to street,
and passing women pause.

Today's the City Show. He lifts the gleam of medallions
around the neck of his Suffolk Shire,

polishes every muscle below the Shire's
black skin, revealing to all who have eyes to see

his own unseen magnificence.
Tomorrow he'll be lifting barrels again from cart

to street, the Shire's flanks reflecting the light
that shines in autumn rain.

Under the table

The table belonged to Mum and Dad.
The darkness under the cloth
belonged to herself alone.

She was always visited there
in her small room.

Today, an oryx stepped delicately
inside the red cloth, and knelt
by her side.

She waited, breathing carefully.
Then shrank: out of the ground
came something she couldn't explain

or even quite see.
Something using a rabbit's shape
to hide a monstrosity.

She had no voice;
her breath was squeezed away.
*What on earth are you doing
in there?*

The voice brought
mother's furrowed face
and a helpless rage.

The button box

I cycled over to see you each day after school to sit
and not say a word, and have you not say a word to me,
just leaving me be.

I'd take out your button box, letting its waterfall
of metal and bone tumble over my hand,
or finger a tinny tune on your old piano
in the chill of the best front room.

The Mask

When the street lights failed
we listened to lapping and licking
until we felt the river's warm vomit
soaking our feet and snaking inside,

sliding over the carpet and inching up walls
choking out air as it rose
and went on rising.
I thought of dad

asleep in the cellar
as mustard gas silently throttled the air.
I watched as we lost the tables
the chairs the paintings the photos

the books our peace plant
that never flowered.
And I thought of dad once six foot tall
shrunk and losing his life

as the rising tide in his lungs
choked out his air in a silent ward
his husked fierce voice from the mask
You'll be like this one day.

Last Meeting with Mum

We met half-way, on the edge of an endless field
in Somerset, and looked in each other's face.
as if it were for the first time. I loved your eyes.
I wanted more.

A few weeks later my father rang
to tell me you had suddenly, unexpectedly, died.
Now

there are tight rows of wheat
where I wanted to meet you again
half-way.

Opening the Earth

Only below where a bank and ditch of the hill-fort
fall away does anything move, roots tunnelling
down amongst the ancestors for last week's rain.

Grandmother said I must never open the earth
for it would tug itself round me, never letting me go.
But earth is welcoming, it holds the voice of the dead.

This land 1

I have lived myself into this land
where long slow winters
stretch thin over Chesil's reach
and nothing moves

only the mist that slides across
the shore and holds me fast –
and skies, that fall and fall
and seek the sea.

This land 2

I have lived myself into those cobbled yards
in the cold chill of farms, the stooking of wheat

that breathed with field-mouse or shrew,
the island of warmth that wrapped itself
round the old kitchen range.

Can they be there
in that sloping field, in that stone house?

Burton Bradstock

From Dorset hills
to the tea-hut on Burton beach
the land has held wreckers
flint-hunters and tropical seas.

These shouldered hills
turn in my bones
along with the gales, the mist
and the bloody arthritis.

Yellow cliffs rear up:
a toppling depth below
Chesil grumbles and turns its lanky spine,
sieving its stones to the east.

In the cliff where sandstone gave footing
to man, an arrow's leaf of careful flint
fell into my hand. I wondered
would you have liked my face?

Chesil's Reach

Morning holds the long slow sky
of winter, stretched thin over Chesil's Reach.

Between shingle and sky, nothing moves.

Softly, a sea-mist slides across the shore,
its shroud holding me fast.

A country line

No more cuttings embankments
stations Toller Porcorum Powerstock
Loders, no trains that wilfully stop
in between to deliver post,
pick buttercups, or simply
take a rest; halted once

to pick up Georgie Biles,
a shepherd, late for his daughter's wedding,
never late for the lambs.
Only deserted scrublands
of willow-herb dandelion
and occasional whiff of fox
testify to their loss.

But the buttercups remember,
and the foxes too.

Firelight

Fire is the starting point. Its tongues
have gossiped our nights away.
Prometheus may have found fire
but man brought it home.

We have lived with fire for so long.
When evening netted the family in
from gusted fields or lamp-skittered rain,
we sat by its wells of flame,

its valleys that vanished in dark,
staring and listening
to tales of the day out there.
We lost ourselves in the looking.

Rope

Rope snakes round the farm
binding, holding, curbing stock and child.
Blocks of stone from the hills have slid indoors

to lie in cold stone floors.
Ben limps his arthritic bones across their chill
and watches Martha with eyes of flint as she

cuts up time in tiny bits to keep out fear.
Jack, fifteen and useful to Ben, has shut
his rage in a box. The day before Christmas,

early milking done, he comes in for a break.
And judders himself to a halt.
Tangles of rope fill the floor,

and higher up is one big tangle
where Martha hangs. He runs to her,
his shouts too big for the room.

Martha's shape moves gently, without reply.

He shrinks himself down and takes out his eyes.
There's nothing left but to make what he can
of an inconsequential life.

The Chesil's narrow throat

Kicking at stones
Joseph trails us along
the Chesil's narrow throat

till it chokes on its dunes;
Andy releases his body
and also his hate
in a tumbling roll
down the dunes.

Above the mile long
bank, sea kale's fleshy
vigour hustles pebbles
aside.

Andy and I collect
skimmers, laugh at
bum-shaped pebbles,
and shout.

Pebbles soften to shingle
so we lie back and look up
at a buzzard circling
lost from its hills.

We remember
family picnics with chips
and bottles of beer.
Joseph has left us

to sit by the cliffs
in his well of dark
and look at the sand.
I can't quite see his face
that is so like hers.

Creator

Monday. God's week has begun.

Craftsmen working among the birds
above Early English naves
crouched over headlong space
longing for flight
created mischievous creatures
with wings and arms
trapping them safely in sleeping stone.
Sat back in builders' cradles and admired.

Not art but I, Creator.

You and I
after Erich Fried

How is it that you
seeing this I
find me so strong
and giving

while I
knowing this I for so long
know myself
worried and weak

and I
knowing and loving you
find you noble
and kind

while you
considering this you
say you aren't
either of these –

how shall we
so deluded
leap this gap?

Promises

Hand over hand I spidered down
the cliff to the sea that sucks at its base;
and found full-breasted Aphrodite playing
and waiting for men of the human race.

She promised me love everlasting
and hot blue skies.
I ran off to the cold Atlantic
where mermaids called from rocks

that slid with ice and seashore wrack,
lay in the chill of its waves
as the fair and generous Hera offered me
power over men and women, life

everlasting and warm blue seas.
I swam away in the cold and heavy
Atlantic waves and called to the
mermaids who lie below in a green

that is nearly black. They sent me tall
Athena who lay with me, pledging a hero's
brave death. I swam to the shore, and lay
like a porpoise beached and ready to die.

A human woman came by, stopped
and promised me nothing but one short life
and problems to grey my hair. Astonished
by belief, I am still here.

Nineteen sixty

For Peter

You'd know the post can be late
even by years. Still, you'll be surprised,
you'd need a walk in your tidy garden,
turning the parcel around
in your thin, ageing hands.

Laura will wonder silently, and watch.
Take care with the torn wrappings
and labels to REDIRECT. The date
is half rubbed out – nineteen sixty x.

My words once bombarded the pots and pans
in an unkempt house: protest marches
and books had seized my days.

You who found stillness in a wood
made shelves to give them a shrine.

The sand-pit's beyond the lawn.
You know who's there.

These things I took away,
with others that wanted to happen
and were refused.

In shock I find
these images I thought
were safely dead
are alive and they are ours.
Fragments to paste into sense
in a different frame.

I'm posting it from then
to the place where you are now.
I'll walk with it incomplete
to the box's red silent mouth
and push it, slowly, inside.

Equinox

The old sun arcs low
days briefly stutter

and shiver

A voice sings on the river
a herring gull screams

and dies.

Tomorrow
daybreak

will open early.

Streets rouse the sky
a boy flings by

on a bike.

An image of Kerry

At two-forty-eight by my watch
the little white sheep jumped suddenly down
on the tussocks of marram grass
bending down to the Kerry waves.

My friend rushed out to know if I'd caught
this Irish thing, a sheep on top of a wall,
in the mobile's store of Images of Kerry.
She herself had stuck pins in dead moths.

I saw a sheep, I said. *I looked and I let it go.*
Neither itself nor its image will tell me
what happens from Now to Then.

I looked at the empty wall, the unburdened air.

Like a small coffin

Winter trees suited you,
their thin limbs angled like elbow or wrist,
drafting your own spiky frame.

Your angles fitted
the hospital bed but its narrowness
thinned you away.

I remember
the day we found
that twenties' gramophone
in its long mahogany coat.
You loved the crackle and boom
of its ancient voice.
Lid down, it looked exactly like
a small coffin laid on its end.

Helle

Yesterday
I saw her on the hillside
scrambling awkwardly among blackberries
happy and pink and scratched.
Today she is dead.

Death came in a sudden rush
unhampered by regulations or pain.
I so wanted her to live some more
but she has gone.

Rift

How did this rift come about
between your words and
my listening?
When you rang

on a day that was once tomorrow,
your voice somehow changed –
I had no way to understand
the word goodbye

till I dug up the past
and found it flourishing there
like a weed
growing and growing

That day

Later that day we stagger
across the deaf shingle,
our voices hounded by wind.

We slide and fall up the drowning steeps
and top them ten paces apart. Stand facing,
duellists waiting for guns.

Dropping abruptly to ground,
you offer me sex here and now –
your instant cure. I refuse;

you spit out venom –
I must be getting it somewhere else.
The gulls scream bitter betrayal

I pick up a dented can of Coke;
I pitch the bent can on the shoreline's wrack,
and leave without a look.

The Letter

A landing flanked by door. A handle invites
and forbids   My fingers are clutching the words
that will halt your frantic rages. Invitation to go.

I touch the wood of our door and remember
a day in Lucca. Grief cements me to ground.
You are sitting small on our bed, hunched

as I found you once over a Singles magazine,
searching its promises for perfect trust.
You look at my hand and wait.

Looking back

You were my continent
my land filled with hills and herons
my unplanned town
its buildings conceived in amazement
its markets filled with fruits and expectations
its streets of opened windows and hopeful doors.

Slowly, over a time
empty boxes piled over market stalls
buildings crumbled and could not be reconstructed
and doors hung empty, unfulfilled.

I have no idea
how this happened
or how to start myself again.

Repossession

From door to garden

I tread out and touch, smell the evergreen air
run my hand along rough wood behind the jasmine.
I did not expect to see you, silent there in the arbour.

Windows second storey may be safe.

I wonder if you're still in the arbour.
I remember that last birthday meal.
You can be silent for hours.

Top windows

present a neighbourhood open to sky.
Garden tables and wine; a boy, an old man, and a ball.
Rooftops, chimneys and rows of windows.
It is all so distant, uninvolved.

You have been gone for two months now.
This house is for me to order, imagine, and rearrange
as I decide. I walk from the curtainless window
of our room and down the stairs.

Old

Something evil comes this way.
I think of being twelve and not wanting
breasts, but now it's a different lynching
in bone and brain, sagging
and grinding *my god, not you again.*

I rage, not at the ending of days –
I'm only just out of my depth
but I can no longer prevail.
Trespassed by anxious mouths
in hard black seas

I'm treading water,
treading and looking
for that one shingle bar I need
to touch down, thrust time away.
There's a ship over there, so I'll wave

but it ploughs steadily on,
like sons and daughters loving
but living in distant times.

Water, drowned in light
After Turner at Tate Britain

The wind is tossing sulky Thames water
across the road and into my hair,
freezing my neck, filling my eyes with tears.

Turner has wrenched me inside out.
His 'Storm' has lashed sea in my face
I'm wet as a cabin-boy on his drowning ship.

Along the winter river, sun is fusing with mist
till I see only light: I know it's light I can touch
if I wait on Vauxhall Bridge.

No-name boy

Scrawny and small he came running,
shouting bad words in a voice twice his size.
He kicked her hard on the shin and ran.

Fury limped her indoors to cold farmhouse
for comfort and treatment of wounds.
There was no-one.

No-one to call her brave soldier.
No-one at all.

They have nothing, said dad –
and at Christmas he told her
grudging hands to send them toys
that were not yet unloved.

They kick, she thought,
and sulked.

A good boy

Grandad, salesman in tiny toys and Christmas decorations,
was one of the undeserving poor. He watched his money
run off in surprising streams between fingers and thumb.

Charlie, fourteen and dandelion bitter, worked with fury
and topped the list for the County Grammar.
Grandad said, 'Charlie, find a job, we need the money now.'

In 1914, when Kitchener needed YOU in his Great War
Charlie went out to Passchendael. He failed to be
blown to bits, came home and started a lifelong sentence.

Tied to a desk, supporting a family. He'd always been
a good boy.

Home again

Waking once again in the tall house,
we think of its unexpected welcome,
its hundreds of books like children,
dangling their legs over shelves
and holding out hands.

We lean on open windows where dawn,
head down and hands in pockets,
stumbles in past coffee and toast.
There's a string of white stars
outside on the arbour roof,
forgiving our trespasses.

Bed-time story

'I think I'm bleeding,' he said
as I put him to bed. So I comforted him,
flew with him to dragons and dinosaurs,

and a giant who took off his head
as you might an unwanted hat.
As he slept I went back to the sofa

and evening TV. By the fruit-vendor's stall,
blood soaks into the ground. His head lies
thrown aside, a fruit no longer for sale.

Half-past four

In winter at half-past four the room is getting dark
I look through the pile of paper handkerchiefs
packs of biscuits and crisps.

Below the table
a pile of bricks, a small bench upside down.
Cardboard boxes, a stick picked up in the woods.

Look closer
the bench turns into a boat or a baby's cradle
boxes slide into hats and housing estates, bricks

grow into palaces, garages and garden walls.
The stick walks down the stairs banging the bannisters
creating a satisfying, annoying noise.

I am come home from school.

Please, Mrs. Beeton, not so many eggs

In the early hours before breakfast
I need words like inquisitive worms,
some with silver coins on their tails.

In the silence before the evening meal
I don't need waterfalls
a few drips
from the kitchen tap will do.

The Old Women

There were so many old women
quietly waiting
they had no need to push for a place

nor make long necklaces of words,
they were not immensely wise
nor bearers of ancient tradition

they grew beans and peas
in orderly rows in gardens
laid out

as they laid out their lives
in manageable lengths
bordered with hedges to keep out

unmanageable hope.

On Dartmoor

Bracken is growing through Dartmoor's ancient stones,
bringing laughter among the gods of the underworld.
Children are chasing the light of the early sun

as it runs after clouds across the grass;
they shriek to see how fast it snatches itself away.
Sunlight weighs so little

as it slides down banks and under branches
that dip in the river's sky. The sun looks up
past pale green weed at the latest rivergod sitting

calculating how many rivers and streams
will make enough rain. What's enough?
A butterfly settles and goes, a robin watches a spade.

Gargoyle

I was born in his head, and trapped in stone
with hammer and blade. He set my mouth
thick-lipped in a perfect O to gather dust.

Then into the hole of my mouth
he took my tail, and high in his church
he set me between two common angels.

Winged, I stared at the crowded congregation.
Looking up, they would nudge a neighbour,
point at my arse. And I up here, all alone.

Glastonbury

Tents, like up-ended cups
each containing a bit of flood.
Mobiles
along with last night's drinks and condoms
are off down the river-road.
Can't find tickets, wallet or even
keys.
Sun's out again
there's some change in my pocket
let's just wade down for a drink.

Green Man

In the twisting of root and rock
in the darkness of trees
you bloom unbidden
and urgent for space.

In the curtly cropped trees
around the town where
your wildwood grew,
you are dead, and we can rest.

But you grow under root and rock
inside my brain, you bloom
unbidden, and urgent for space.

Miss Peat

Below your dismissive eye
is the undisturbed, disturbing
country of nearby.
Sit in a siding, a layby, the grass
at the quarry's edge –
and use whatever's around.

Last night's storm
that walked you home,
dark green figs in a row
the spaces where we don't talk.

Even Miss Peat
on the motorway verge
in her picnic chair
wearing a tired hat
and a frightened face,
a long way from Walthamstow.

Becoming
after Francis Bacon

Paint breaks down Velasquez' Pope
the one with leashed furious eyes
breaks all bodies down

a glistening spread
of components, blood and entrails,
paint shining and crucifying
bodies always becoming
paint smearing away the possibility
of ending
paint seeking a way out
of the frame.

Homeless

1

Windows close
night settles down
on city roofs and on strangers
  who walk alone.

Streets lie in wait.
With cold intimacy
they importune
  as you walk.

A green square huddles
seats murmur and cough
a stranger space for your bed
  light cloud overhead.

2 The Boy

After my dad was dead
Mum lost her mind
Someone must leave she said
You're old enough.

I shut my head and walked.
The streets circled round.

I wanted to batter at doors.
At night I shook

for dad who was dead.
Tried to unzip myself
and die like him
on the flagstone bed.

but here are two men
*   bringing sandwiches*
and hot cups of tea

3pm at The Craven Arms

It's Scuddy, George and Micky, their red cheeks blowing –
the Roaring Boys who brought the sixties to town
and rode with the devil pillion on their bikes. The boys
who'd never get piles or arthritis, and never die.

Side by side in the Craven Arms they're staring
straight ahead, hatching a roomful of words
that stagger and fall They ride their stories round
and back till the rubber's worn off the rim.

The barman dowses the lights.
The three of them lock
together, rise as one.
Gentlemen, says Scuddy, *shall we go?*

Poetry Seminar

Squirrels, we skittered through words and phrases,
looked at their colours and hoarded their random
shine for times when nothing moved.

Your words – pinpoint, exact – scattered among us,
caught by a sideways glance or left to lie.
Unbothered, you offered more,

till one or other of us picked up a word
that astonished, pushing thought aside
and leading a vagabond into the heart.

Not Myself

The sun is moving my shadow
around the room. In my hand
is my blue and white cup;

this is my after-lunch tea.
The black cat with his angry nose
is on the window ledge

in his usual way. But the door
is not my door. Out there
is not my garden. I am not myself.

Where is the purple belled clematis,
the jasmine that John didn't like,
and when did he die?

High Dependency Ward

Also called Level One.
It had no other name
for its pain.

In beds One Two and Three
bodies flat and white
lay hulked without engine,
wired and tubed to
things that measured, that dripped
or flowed.
Their eyes swallowed space.

Number Four
was a head that slept
an open mouth
a table with uneaten food
and frequent scurrying curtains.

Number Five
for no apparent reason
sat up in his bed
and remembered he had a name.

Sacrifice

Consider us, your ancestors.
We took an axe to the neck
of one man. Quickly.
Buried him in a bog

to make sure the sun
would rise as before
and rain would fall
on crops.

*

Calvary. Crucifixion. Nailed
and hung up to bleed. Muscles
and lungs collapsing until
he's unable to breathe.

That was his side of the bargain
you made with your god.
After this sacrifice, your god
would forgive his people their sins.

All of them.

*

You call us barbarians.

Fishing

A rod that whips, attacks the air
precisely, calculated
just there,
on that particular spot

and drops.
Float settles in, shrugs with
water's gentle undulations.
It's an unruffled day.

He sighs and sits,
satisfied for now,
thinks of Jesus who fished for men
and feels good.

Stares at clouds and trees
in the river, twisted by passing boats.
He's had rare encounters here.
Father O'Ferris, who died

last year, so loved
and so very familiar
when he was thirteen;
who'd left his habitation

inside the throat of a crow
and cast himself
into these lonely waters.

Mackerel eyes

I see the mackerel march off
their slab in militant array.
The fishmonger's hand

pounces forth. *This one, lady?*
I watch as mackerel slides
and beats beneath his hand.

Well, almost. I touch his skin.
'It's still alive.' You stupid woman.
He grins. *Dead long before you*

got up today, I reckon.
I am watching mackerel eyes
as they meet mine.

You want it, or not?

Hours 1

Hours need space to swim round, to grow fat in the sun
at noon, or thin when the air cracks with cold.

Hours belong to a tree that hunches its back to the wind.

Hours 2

Hours don't walk arm in arm with sunlight,
moon and harvest any more.
They live in a queue of empty boxes,
waiting to be used.

You fill an empty hour with breakfast,
a kiss that barely smudges the air.
We use our separate hours distantly.
I wish we did not.

Multiverse

She met atoms and nuclei rather late in life.
Just another family, expecting her to revolve
around their outskirts. She was used to that.

Also no great surprise to be told that she was
mostly space inside; that's how she saw
herself. In the Uni bar, she met

a small group of particles. 'We are virtual,'
they said, as they flickered in and out.
They talked of a trillion million universes,

all there by unpredictable, random chance.
She knew that already, she said. Since two,
she'd failed completely to find any links

between what she said and did, and the casual,
usually nasty, results. Now she could see
she was in the wrong universe, had slipped

from her proper part of the multiverse.
To comfort her, they spoke with awe
of the stupendously massive Higgs Bosun;

she longed for mass, its dignity. But was the
HB just massive, or lumpily obese?
'We were told', they said after heated talk,
'someone called SUSY leads a virtual dance

around HB, with squarks and their quarky twins,
also sleptons and leptons, photinos and photons,
to stop him getting fat.'

She'd looked for a different family since she was
ten, but really, she thought with some indignation,
it might be wiser to pass this one up.

Oh ye of little faith

The view is brown to the knees and
the postman won't come
through the gate.

It's a wicked world down there,
says the Fisherman sideways sly.
Hop in the boat. We row into

Market Square, and past the salmon
that leap and shine in the shallows inside
the grocer's shop. The Fisherman

looks up at the hill where better folk lie
in their dry and gated groups.
He eyes the lowering clouds and scowls

till they drop and the hill is blotted in rain.
A flood-watching group by the gates
rush to rescue their tablecloths wine and

a couple of Baskerville hounds.
Hang on a sec says the Fisherman, while
I shift the floods a bit. He closes his eyes

and I swear the waters move *up* the hill
and through the gates. The Fisherman
grins and fingers his curly beard.

Herb Robert

You said you don't do belonging;
you didn't pretend.
I didn't hear your words.
I loved the smell of your skin.

I loved.
You almost stayed (and you almost left)
for almost eleven years.

You only managed to go
when you suddenly died.
Your absence smells as bitter

as that small flower herb robert,
and as familiar. Perhaps it's only
the hillside where your ashes fell.

The two of you

You were a vibrant plant with jagged leaves
and spikes. You died. The spikes
still slash at me and I want to tear you out
and shred you, flush you away.

Only one problem. We fucked
so sublimely. Tender and springing
you opened me right out
as we dissolved laughter in love.

So when I sit on the sofa, the end that droops
where you habitually sat, memory splits.
Did you just slam the door yelling
leave me alone

or are we sprawled on the landing laughing,
licking and scrambling for ways to get in?
After you died I thought I'd find
love without spikes

but you left me unwrapped
the two of you fighting inside
while memory bucked and ripped
as I tried to shut the door.

Dungeness

Abandoned huts and machines
taunt us with images
of a past that worked.

We could not grasp
the tentative kindnesses
of spring.

At the sea's edge, a last
fishing smack prevaricates,
seduces our dreams.

Here in the centre,
an anchor protrudes
from dry stones, securing
nothing.

Blackbird

The sun and I
are stretched out in my garden.
I'm sinking inside the stones
as if this opiate warmth were slowly
dissolving body and brain.

A fluster of wings as the local
blackbird lands in my space
three feet away at the water's edge
and stops with gimlet eyes on me,
ready for flight.

He stays for a bath:
then a flash like sun on glass,
a whirr –
he's gone, taking his world
that can't stay long in mine.

I think of my father, whose ways
were quiet and still and full of trees,
and my mother,
who'd once loved to dance,
folding herself inside a porcelain shell

And you, my love – like the blackbird
always ready to leave – but only
managing it when you suddenly died.

Stranger in his own head

Our son is thirteen. Deceived by the dark,
he sleeps, shifting his mind to another place.
Bewildered by your death, he comes alone

to the river's edge where he saw you die,
your eyes seeking his as you fell. He hears
minute spills of sound as ground begins

to form frost. Hours loosen; night lies cold
on the hill. The river is molten lead, its waters
heavy and slow. He watches you rise each night,

breaking the thick meniscus that held you until
you drowned. He says you seem surprised that
he is there, alone in the darkness and chill.

Slithering

Out on a rooftop, slates are flaring wet
and I think something's slithering there
inside the tiles.
Here you are
telling me it's a flat grey day and nothing
happens. I look at you and think
maybe I'm inside out.

The rain lines up in drops
under the sycamore's arm,
so I wait to see. Nothing happens.

If I stand and watch,

something
may slither into my mind.

Oceans

In oceans' midnight zone
where there's no light to make food
it is neither good nor bad
to eat each other.

At dusk
the well-known Bathyscaphoid Squid
tanks up on ammonium ions
to get that buoyant feeling
that nothing else can give.

He joins that restless group
the Dancing Siphonophores
and their billions of silent followers
who rise from the midnight sea
to a solar-powered feast,
riding back home at dawn.

Among them, down in the smoky murk
of a basement ridge, you may find
those druggies the tube-worms
shrimps and clams taking
their thermochemical fix
from eager bacteria dodging and dancing
round brines from spouting volcanic vents.

You know the far side of the moon better than you know us.

Fish

Walls of stone draw November's chill
from the river; they slide it deep indoors.
He barrels fish by fish into winter's salt,

layer by layer, spokes of a wheel.
His child rushes eager shovels
across the floor, spilling white streams.

Firm and flat, they drown in rivers
of salt, scales dulled to brown and grey.
She wants them to protest,

to flash up and out to the river
that flows in November air and light.
She walks out to stand in the falling leaves.

Sarratt, 1944

Bare legs steady in water, head bending
and hands dipped, a boy is stroking trout.
A meadow, a stand of summer trees.

The Immigrants' Child

She looks round the room, now cleared of all
they'd brought with shameful care from over the sea.
Only their pictures remain. The man and woman

so carefully photographed had long since moved on.
A wind of panic stirs.
She isn't there, in the way their pictures are there.

Who am I? I am Mary, my mother Mary's child.

No. I belong to no-one. I am whoever I like.
She wants to lift up her words like a quilt to see
who's there beneath.

Lurking

Only the children know how open the borders are,
how easily transgressed.

So the outsiders come in, smelling of earth and wet,
playmates covered in dark.

Four-legs waits in the kitchen behind the sink.
He knows that lurking helps bring up the animal

inside his skin. The creeping through bush
and briar, sniffing the earth and the night

and knowing again the biting pleasure of smell
roots and bodies and burial.

A black crow mutters, a fox coughs in the wood.

The Woods are Listening

In the silence of early air the woods are listening
for voices they lost without remembering when,
though it was, they know, before the first angels grew their wings.

There was nothing else to do so long ago under the empty sky
but wait and listen to passing planets.
The trees remember the shift as they moved away and the air sighed.

The voices came from a sky that was dark as black.
Perhaps they were there to look after travellers
who never arrived.

The voices dropped slowly down into the trees,
and gossiped like friends in the night.

Today

The years have numbers now;
I am surprised to find I shall not
be here forever, familiar and known.

The hills are unaware of
the trackways I climb, the woods
indifferent to the paths I walk.

A fox pauses, his nose uplifted
as wood smoke furls briefly by.
I walk on to where you wait
at the bend in the path.

The Witch

In winter-dark river
lie trees, twisting and cracked
by the water's long axe.
I lounge in reflection's deceits:

I swing with the currents below
considering my mortality
the fox barks chill in seeping winter mist
and stands spark-halted, foot in pause
as nose reads a signalling air

I breathe and live in his jaws
closing, crunching, tearing.
The crow carries me shaking
through his fractured canto of death

I glimmer in skylark's startled surge.
Uninvited, I trespass in your head.
I walk your tangled paths of thought
and map your dreams.

Where lust wears fragile gowns
I leap my mind in yours
and know you well
Today, they whisper as I pass

and say I see too much;
I have one eye, but I live
in a world of two-eyed fools
who fear to see.

Becoming and vanishing

Light slides behind the tiles
as if some animal or fish
were just beneath the surface
becoming and vanishing.

As in a mirror I watch
my mother's face slide
beneath my skin
almost but not clearly seen,
becoming and vanishing.

Today and tomorrow

And then there is the void between today
and the filling in of tomorrow.

Can you see the last flash of today over there
as it blinks and blurs out of view?

There, on the very point of Portland Bill –
the cliff's thronging with people who shout

and wave as they try to lasso tomorrow

Special Things

There are only two handles left
on the old kitchen chest of drawers.

So I've lost track of my special things:
the saffron the cumin my bondage bra
and the green gunpowder tea, also
the scarlet knickers somewhere
down to the left, and the Amour de Nuit.

The sun binges on every day,
the evergreens hum on one note,
squalled out by acid jazz and razzle
from macaws and parrots with
syncopations from next door's wailing goat.

Every Friday night after work
he brings home a bunch of roses,
a bottle of dry white wine.
And he says my God, what a week.
Every time.

Sun and the booze have kippered me
and crêped up my skin, and I think this is us,
this is it. I'm leaving today to be an old biker's
favourite doll. Next Friday night at the door
he'll call out, *Anyone home?*

Lost Hilltop

It's our hilltop, has been for years.
We walk, and talk ourselves back to familiarity,
scissored by winds that have blown us from childhood to age.

We stumble and stop. Seduced by remembered familiarity,
we had wandered at ease till a gathering mist had removed
all our landmarks.

A stranger, treading firmly, loomed up face
to face. His eyes were amused. 'Be you lost?'
he asked. 'I'll take thee back to the car-park,

shall I?' Consolingly he went on.
'You need to know this hilltop very well before
you wander. You'll be strangers, I expect.'

The Single Track

You said our wedding day closed down the track
you'd run alone and free in all your years,
unhurt by lover's rage or tears –
you wished you'd known that in the wedding pack

was fractious compromise and blame,
a hedge of words that pierce your head,
a daily toil that saps the joys of bed
and shuts the lid on hope's unwary game.

And yet – around a sudden bend the glance
of sun on sea; the hill flares out to light.
High up, we watch a buzzard's solo flight.
You wonder if you might give things a chance.

Some days you walk along a single track.
I hold your hand a while when you get back.

Old Age

It can start almost anywhere.
For my wife it was plumbing and drains;
for me it's the framework,

the beams the uprights and joists
that crumble away inside, unnoticed
for years. I had them underpinned

and some of them replaced;
they tinkered until the tinkerings
gave way. Could I be like Margaret,

berating rural railway stations for ramps
to lift her collapsing undercarriage
gently inside the train?

Could I do that?

To George Melly
Jazz musician, television and radio personality

It is not possible for you to be
dead. The concept's ridiculous.
Here you are
spending yourself in fireworks and colour
all over streets and stage
the original random particle
leaping to wave-
like form

finally interrupted
in the red hat
collided
in blazers built for a bus
gone, exploded –
George
        George
thank you for existing.

Self-portrait, George Romney

Something vital
he's left unsaid.
I look in his eyes
alive with a need
that's waited two hundred years
for someone who'll see.
I stand transfixed
I cannot move on
he's looking directly at me.

The Travellers

They'd walked too fast, arriving
frayed and thrown about.
Something missing.

In all that haste,
they'd left their souls behind.
The travellers sat by the water,

waiting until they caught up.
Stayed, till each found the right one.
The careful tucking in, to settle them.

Catching up

As I sag into sleep the clocks go ticking east
and the west comes scurrying after,
tic tic tic too late, too late

click
and the gate is shut.
Yet clocks do sleep

leaving grandad with one grave ear open
for those who leave with the skimming longitudes
I am old, I could   tic   and stop.

He could be away when I leave
the clocks going tic tic tic and the hours
carried helplessly east for a day and a night.

Maps

I lift a handful of sand,
hot and dry.
Down there in my shadowed scoop,
one tiny grain moves uncertainly.
It has legs. Without a microscope
I cannot see how many.

I shall call the creature Sid.

Sid gathers speed,
but he must go round obstacles.
An obstacle is anything larger than
a grain of sand.

He weaves a very long path, that looks
erratic, but is probably
well planned. It takes minutes
to travel an inch.

My friend has a magnifier.
We examine Sid more closely;
find that he carries something hooked
by one leg.
He stops every now and then,
holding the something erect.

It is now perfectly clear:
Sid is mapping his terrain.

It occurs to my friend and me
that the coastline of Britain
will now – if Sid is accurate –
be several million miles long.

The Ordinance Survey
will not approve at all.

But which of them is Right?